# BLESSED IS THE MAN WHO TRUSTS IN THE LORD

*For he will be like a tree planted by the water*

## 25 DEVOTIONS FOR MEN

Kenneth Wagener

*Blessed Is the Man Who Trusts in the Lord*
by Kenneth Wagener

www.CTAinc.com

Copyright © 2007 CTA, Inc.
1625 Larkin Williams Rd.
Fenton, MO 63026-1205

Scripture quotations are taken from the HOLY BIBLE, NEW INTERNATIONAL VERSION®. Copyright © 1973, 1978, 1984 International Bible Society. Used by permission of Zondervan. All rights reserved.

PRINTED IN THAILAND

*Blessed is the man who trusts in the LORD,*
*whose confidence is in him.*
*He will be like a tree planted by the water*
*that sends out its roots by the stream.*
*Jeremiah 17:7–8*

Through faith, God promises, you are blessed. He has
poured out his grace on you, and he now considers
you his beloved son because of the death and resurrection
of Jesus Christ.

Look at yourself as a man of faith whose life goal is to be a
mighty tree planted in the fertile, well-watered soil of God's love.
That's how Jeremiah describes you in the verses above. That's good
news as you live as a Christian in your family, daily work,
community, and church.

Start your devotional time each day with this prayer. Reflect on
how your Lord has called you. And to cultivate your growth in
his Word, read and pray about the Scripture passage in
"Deeper and Higher."

### A Prayer Based on Jeremiah 17:7–8

Lord, you call me blessed. And so I am.
Call me your son again now, as I rest in your
fatherly care and *begin/end* this day.

Lord, I pray for myself . . . Plant me firmly in rich soil as I trust in
you. Let my roots go out far and wide, so that I may stand tall as a
man of faith in your world. Let my confidence in your Word grow
deeper and higher as you ground me in your truth and establish
me in your love. I especially ask . . . *Pray the Lord's guidance
on your beliefs and attitudes, your character, your talents
and skills, your management of his gifts, and your service
to his church.*

Lord, I pray for others . . . May they thrive in faith, growing
green leaves and plentiful fruit, even in the hot, dry seasons
of life. I especially ask . . . *Pray God's strength and wisdom for
your family, for all your relationships, for work and neighborhood
commitments, and for your witness to Christ.*

Lord, I pray for your help in a day of trouble . . . *Pray God's grace
and healing for temptation and pressure to conform, for loss and
hardships, for health concerns and conflict resolution, for yourself
and others.*

Make me stand strong and sturdy, Lord. Grow me every day in
your grace, as I bless your holy name. Amen.

*Blessed is the man who trusts in the LORD,*
*whose confidence is in him.*
*Jeremiah 17:7*

God has planted you.

You are the tree of his choosing,
   the man he has designed
   and called you to be.

He is growing you deeper and higher,
   that you may be blessed and
   that he may be glorified in everything,
   to the praise and honor of Jesus Christ.

# The Planter

*Now the LORD God had planted a garden in the east, in Eden; and there he put the man he had formed. (Genesis 2:8)*

How did those tulip oak trees come to stand in the middle of your yard? How did that grove of cedars come to rim your property?

Most likely you planted them. Or perhaps the developer who created your subdivision. Then again, perhaps they grew tall and straight long before you—or anyone else—purchased your home or acreage and moved in. Even then, the truth is that someone planted those trees.

You know who! Your God. Your God is a planter. *The* planter of all creation. Don't miss the grace and power of God's character in the opening chapters of Scripture. In Genesis 1, God creates. God separates. God gathers. God causes trees and plants to grow. God crafts lights in the sky. God fashions and sends forth fish and birds and mammals. God creates it all—everything you see in this vast, magnificent planet called Earth.

And then the climax of his creation: "Now the Lord God had planted a garden in the east, in Eden; and there he put the man he had formed." A perfect conclusion to the work of his hands. God is the master gardener.

Take another look at God the planter. He's planted you. Put you right where he wants you to stand, right where he wants you to mature. Placed you right where he wants to use you for his purposes. Your Father has created you and re-created you in Jesus Christ to be "the man who trusts in the LORD, whose confidence is in him" (Jeremiah 17:7).

The devotional readings in this book will guide you into the prophet Jeremiah's faithful words from the Lord to you, the man he has formed by his perfect plan. Each day you'll explore the grace and power of God's presence and purpose in your life. You'll discover how God is calling and equipping you to be a tree rooted and refreshed in his love in Christ.

He's planted you to be evergreen and bear fruit. You are blessed!

### Deeper and Higher
Consider how God looks at you:

*They will be called oaks of righteousness,*
*a planting of the LORD*
*for the display of his splendor.*

Isaiah 61:3

## Planted for His Blessing

*Then God said, "Let us make man in our image, in our likeness,
and let them rule over the fish of the sea and the birds of the air,
over the livestock, over all the earth, and over all the creatures
that move along the ground." (Genesis 1:26)*

Have you noticed? The Bible honors you as God's special
creation. As he did with Adam, your Father made you
individually. He fashioned you uniquely in his divine image
and likeness and set you apart as his representative, his delegate
in his world. You, too, have authority to rule over the work of
his hands.

But something else marks you as God's special creation. With
fire in his heart and mind, Jeremiah declares, "Blessed is the man
who trusts in the LORD, whose confidence is in him" (17:7).

You are doubly blessed. God has made you alive again. He has
re-created you for a new and living relationship with himself.
He has refashioned your sinful self by grace and now shaped
you into the image and likeness of his perfect Son, Jesus Christ.
Through Jesus you now believe in our Creator God, and your
confidence rests in the Father who richly and daily forgives,
renews, and empowers you to live as a man of faith in your
world. As a man of faith in all your relationships. As a man
of faith in all your work.

You are a man who trusts in the Lord. And he has planted you
to be a blessing to your world—to all the people he has planted
in your life.

What will you invest in your relationships today? Think deeply about honoring the people close to your heart—a spouse, a parent, a son or daughter, or a friend. Ask your Father for insight and wisdom. Then thank him for the people he has placed in your life.

### Deeper and Higher

Remember that God is making you new today—individually and in your relationship with others:

*You have taken off your old self with its practices*
*and have put on the new self,*
*which is being renewed in knowledge*
*in the image of its Creator.*
*Colossians 3:9–10*

## Planting the Future

*"For I know the plans I have for you," declares the LORD, "plans to prosper you and not to harm you, plans to give you hope and a future." (Jeremiah 29:11)*

Planting is an act of faith. You plant, believing that today is not the end. You trust that tomorrow will arrive and bring new life and new beginnings.

Jeremiah wrote a letter to God's people in exile in Babylon. They'd been taken from their homeland by an enemy king. Now they asked hard, troubling questions: Why go on? Why do anything today when we don't know about tomorrow?

Through his prophet, God answered Israel: "Build houses and settle down; plant gardens and eat what they produce. Marry and have sons and daughters; find wives for your sons and give your daughters in marriage, so that they too may have sons and daughters. Increase in number there; do not decrease" (Jeremiah 29:5–6).

God was planting his tomorrow. He planted through the children and grandchildren of this generation. He had plans for his people—"to prosper you and not to harm you, plans to give you hope and a future" (29:11).

Are you planting hope and a future in your children? Or in the lives of children around you—nephews and nieces, grandsons and granddaughters, the boys and girls in your neighborhood or church?

Think back to the men who have shaped and mentored you in the past. They planted seeds—seeds of faith, hope, love—in your mind and heart. They cultivated a harvest—a harvest of goodness, gentleness, and other fruit of the Spirit—in your life. They invested in your today so that you might pass on a spiritual legacy for someone else's tomorrow.

What lasting things will you plant today, trusting the Lord to make them grow?

### *Deeper and Higher*
God's reminder to you:

*See how the farmer waits for the land
to yield its valuable crop and how patient he is.
. . . You too, be patient and stand firm.*
James 5:7–8

## Planting with Purpose

*So neither he who plants nor he who waters is anything,
but only God, who makes things grow. The man who plants
and the man who waters have one purpose, and each will be
rewarded according to his own labor. (1 Corinthians 3:7–8)*

Buyouts. Outsourcing. Downsizing. These are the words that
describe today's workplaces.

Years ago, most jobs had the life cycle of trees. You were planted
on a farm or in a factory or at an office. You grew there; you
flowered and ripened and retired where—or close to where—
you began. But not so today.

Even if you are relatively young in your career, you've likely been
uprooted and replanted at least once. Or trimmed back. Or
perhaps you feel like you've been cut down and tossed aside to
make room for other trees—younger, fresher, more colorful or
distinctive. Maybe you're no longer firmly rooted, and you're
restless to find a workplace where you can sink your roots down
deep and begin—more securely and consistently—to bear fruit.

What meaning does work have in today's competitive, global economy? What meaning does *your* work have? Does it mean anything at all? God says, Yes! Your work has purpose—whatever it is—because God has called you to it. 1 Peter 4:10 tells us, "Each one should use whatever gift he has received to serve others." He is working through you. He is working with you and in you to make his world grow and flourish.

As you go about your daily tasks, varied as they may be, you are planting and watering. You work, but ultimately God gives the growth. He has planned your work—past, present, and future—and he promises to give you the wisdom and strength you need to carry out his purposes for you.

You can trust your Father to guide you as you go about your tasks today. You can call on him for focus and drive when you meet challenges and setbacks. Then watch him bless the results as you put your confidence in Christ.

## Deeper and Higher
Stand firm in the promise God makes to you:

*Let nothing move you.*
*Always give yourselves fully to the work of the Lord,*
*because you know that your labor in the Lord*
*is not in vain.*
1 Corinthians 15:58

## Planting Better Together

*Two are better than one, because they have a good return for their work: If one falls down, his friend can help him up. But pity the man who falls and has no one to help him up! (Ecclesiastes 4:9–10)*

What do you like to do
with your friends?

Golf?
Fish or hunt?
Visit car shows or take
motorcycle trips?
Attend NASCAR races or use
season tickets to your favorite
pro team's games?
Joke by e-mail or text messaging?

Solomon pictures friends doing something more. In his pointed meditation on life (the book in the Bible named Ecclesiastes), Israel's wise king sees men working side by side, planting, harvesting, building, tearing down, scattering, gathering, waging war, pursuing peace—the whole range of human activities under the sun.

All this happens, he notes, by God's design. The Father sets "a time for everything" (Ecclesiastes 3:1), and he gives men—young and old—the grace and skill to accomplish all their tasks.

Yet "two are better than one." Friends stand together. Friends succeed together. Friends defend themselves together. Friends do together—better together—what they cannot do alone.

Your friends are a gift to you from your Father. He has planted them in your life, perhaps next door, perhaps across the state or country. Wherever they are, God brought you together so that your life—and your faith—would be stronger, richer, more influential than the life you could live "on your own."

The Lord has plans for you and your friends. He wants you to grow—together—to be men of faith, cheering one another on, urging one another upward in the call to live in service to Christ and his church.

Take time for your friends today. Do something! And rest in the confidence that your Father will bless you in it as you grow.

### *Deeper and Higher*
Meditate on your Savior's words of affirmation:

*I have called you friends, for everything that I learned from my Father I have made known to you. You did not choose me, but I chose you and appointed you to go and bear fruit—fruit that will last. Then the Father will give you whatever you ask in my name. This is my command: Love each other.*
*John 15:15–17*

## Who Am I?

*Over the next two days, reflect on the different ways
God is working in your life to draw you closer to himself in
faith and to bless you to be a blessing to others.*

**My Identity as a Man**
**My Relationships**
**The Children in My Life**
**My Work**
**My Friends**

*But blessed is the man who trusts in the LORD,
whose confidence is in him.*
*Jeremiah 17:7*

*He will be like a tree planted by the water
that sends out its roots by the stream.*
**Jeremiah 17:8**

God has planted you in Christ.

Every day he draws you to the Living Water,
who alone will satisfy your thirsty soul.

Let your roots spread out, far and wide,
    as you recognize his blessings in your life.

Set apart the gifts he has entrusted to you,
    and dedicate yourself
    to growing deeper and higher in his Word,
    that all may see Jesus in you.

## Roots

*So then, just as you received Christ Jesus as Lord, continue to live in him, rooted and built up in him, strengthened in the faith as you were taught, and overflowing with thankfulness. (Colossians 2:6–7)*

Go underground. Subterranean. That's where you'll find roots.

Below every grand and sturdy tree, you'll find a remarkable system of roots. Sprawling, twisting, and hidden, roots play vital roles in the life of a tree. Roots anchor the trunk and branches. Roots provide stability when winter winds bluster. Roots absorb nutrients—oxygen and minerals—from the soil. Roots store food—carbohydrates—produced by the tree. Who cares about roots? Only wise and diligent gardeners.

Jeremiah describes you when he writes, "He will be like a tree planted by the water that sends out its roots by the stream" (Jeremiah 17:8). God planted you, and now he desires that you set down roots to anchor and nourish and preserve you as you carry out the work he has in mind for you to do. Think for a moment about your roots—that sprawling, twisting, hidden system of deep beliefs, principles, and attitudes. How would you describe them? In what ways do your roots anchor and nurture you? Now listen to the apostle Paul:

*For in Christ all the fullness of the Deity lives in bodily form, and you have been given fullness in Christ, who is the head over every power and authority. (Colossians 2:9–10)*

You have fullness in Jesus. True God, true man, Christ continually fills you with his life—his crucifixion and resurrection life. He begins that filling at the roots. He begins with the beliefs, principles, and attitudes that flow from your deepest identity as his forgiven, precious son. As you seek him in his Word, you absorb his sacrificial love, his unsurpassed wisdom and truth, his passion for lost men.

Think of Jesus as the wise and diligent gardener who cultivates you to make you strong and overflowing with thankfulness. Let him do his work in you today, his subterranean work.

### *Deeper and Higher*

As you pray today, ask that the Father:

*. . . strengthen you with power through his Spirit in your inner being, so that Christ may dwell in your hearts through faith . . . being rooted and established in love . . . that you may be filled to the measure of all the fullness of God.*
*Ephesians 3:16–19*

## Noble Character

*Now the Bereans were of more noble character than the Thessalonians, for they received the message with great eagerness and examined the Scriptures every day to see if what Paul said was true. (Acts 17:11)*

Maybe you've said it at some point: "That tree has character!"

Some trees stand out from the rest. You notice their unusual shape. Their vibrant colors. Or their intriguing pattern of branches. Trees have *character*. Look closely and you'll discern the qualities and traits that make each one distinctive, each one significant.

For Jeremiah, the "tree planted by the water" has its own cluster of qualities and traits—a character that comes directly from God. The Lord forms it. The Lord shapes it, giving it the exact contour and profile he wishes. God knows what it takes to bring out the vibrant colors. He understands how to cultivate its true character and make it flourish, how to generate ample, sturdy branches. The Lord knows just exactly how he will use this tree to impact his world.

Look closely to discern how God is forming your character as well. You may struggle with relationships at the office. You may worry about retirement years and financial security for your future. You may wrestle with sexual temptations and the call to purity. You may wonder how to communicate with the woman you love.

Through all these challenges, God seeks to shape the true you, to make it possible for you to express outwardly the new inward character he has given you in Christ. His work begins, as the Bereans understood, in his Word.

Through his Word, your Father will make you the distinctive tree he wants you to be. In that Word he reveals your true significance, your true identity as his beloved son, connected in faith to the Beloved Son, Jesus Christ.

As you read and hear the Scriptures, receive God's message with "great eagerness." Open your Bible "every day" to feed the roots of your faith. Let your Father use his Word to shape your character—your noble character in Christ—so that others around you may know his Word is true.

### Deeper and Higher
Be confident in the Lord's promise:

*He who began a good work in you will carry it on to completion until the day of Christ Jesus.*
Philippians 1:6

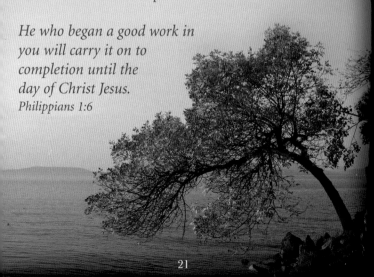

## One Treasure

*Godliness with contentment is great gain. (1 Timothy 6:6)*

Godliness? Certainly. Contentment with one's possessions? Yes, but hard to do in our materialistic society. Both in the same breath? Wow! What a juxtaposition!

Some say, "Let's keep faith and finances in separate corners. Let's put our heavenly riches and our earthly wallets in different back pockets. What God gives us spiritually and what we earn by the sweat of our brow are two unrelated matters." Right?

The man who trusts in the Lord recognizes all God's gifts— including money—as blessings from his hands. A tree planted by water, with roots deep and wide in God's grace, receives God's daily goodness with a spirit of thanksgiving and contentment.

But how about you? Do you trust God with your money? Do you know his will for your finances? As Paul the apostle writes to Timothy, he shares some profound convictions about money and wealth. Ponder the insights he shares as he closes his letter (1 Timothy 6:17–19):

- Though you may be rich in this present world, don't be arrogant or put your hope in earthly wealth. It's all uncertain; you have no guarantee you'll have anything tomorrow—or that you'll be on earth to need it!
- God richly provides us with everything for our enjoyment. He opens his heart and hands and freely gives. Take! Enjoy! Use responsibly.

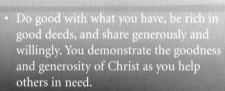

- Do good with what you have, be rich in good deeds, and share generously and willingly. You demonstrate the goodness and generosity of Christ as you help others in need.
- Lay up treasure in heaven, for God has planned your true life with him forever.

By trusting God with your money and finances, you send your roots out far and wide into the fertile soil of thanksgiving and contentment. Whatever comes, you trust your Father will care for you, will provide for you and those you love most.

God gives you one wallet, one pocket . . . to hold everything he gives. All his blessings belong in the same pocket because, after all, it's all one treasure, one pure gift from your heavenly Father. Thank him today for his kindness.

### *Deeper and Higher*
Remember the treasure that Jesus has poured out on you:

*You know the grace of our Lord Jesus Christ,*
*that though he was rich, yet for your sakes*
*he became poor, so that you through his*
*poverty might become rich.*
2 Corinthians 8:9

## Useful to the Master

*Bless all his skills, O LORD, and be pleased with the work of his hands. (Deuteronomy 33:11)*

At the end of his life Moses prayed for his people—for the Israelites. One by one, tribe after tribe, this man of God offered brief yet heartfelt prayers for the men, women, and children he had traveled and lived with from slavery in Egypt to the brink of the Promised Land. Now his death was in sight; time was short. So he turned to his Father to ask a blessing for generations to come.

"Bless all his skills, O LORD," Moses prayed. "Be pleased with the work of his hands."

What skills has God given you? Whatever they are, first recognize them as his gifts. Your talents, your abilities and expertise, learned or natural, all derive from your Father. All your skills, whatever you have, all have come to you unearned, simply by God's grace to you. He has planted them in you, like different kinds of trees in a yard, and has caused each to thrive as you have needed them.

But also be sure to see your skills as tools—God-given tools. You build with tools. You fix with tools. You modify and fine-tune and make things better and more durable with tools.

God uses your skills as tools for his purposes. And he gives you the privilege of offering whatever tools you have—some sharp, some rusty—as the work of your hands to honor him and serve the people he has placed in your life.

Recall again Jeremiah's words: "Blessed is the man who trusts in the LORD, whose confidence is in him" (17:7). Your trust, your confidence are anchored in the Lord. Why not pray that the Lord bless your skills and the work of your hands—for his glory and purposes? Why not pray for your family, your co-workers, your friends and neighbors, that their skills also may be channeled in service to the Lord?

And ask your Father also for work—tool work!—work that will please him and will build and fix and improve your home life and workplace and neighborhood and church. Let him work through you to richly bless others.

### Deeper and Higher
Know that you serve the only King.

*Do you see a man skilled in his work?*
*He will serve before kings.*
Proverbs 22:29

## Gifts of the Spirit

*For in [Christ Jesus] you have been enriched in every way—in all your speaking and in all your knowledge. Therefore you do not lack any spiritual gift as you eagerly wait for our Lord Jesus Christ to be revealed. (1 Corinthians 1:5, 7)*

*Jesus gives gifts to his church. Raised to heaven and ruling over this vast universe, the Lord pours out of heaven's abundance upon his people. The Bible makes it doubly certain. David predicted it, and Paul announced its fulfillment: "When he ascended on high, he led captives in his train and gave gifts to men" (Ephesians 4:8; see also Psalm 68:18).*

Each gift of grace, bestowed and empowered by the Holy Spirit, flows from the crucified and risen Lord. Forgiveness. Peace. Joy. Purpose in life. Comfort in times of pain and loss. Fellowship in the body of Christ. Brotherhood with Christ himself!

In addition to all this, Jesus has also given you spiritual gifts—not just attitudes and skills, but supernatural abilities—to be used to support and unify the body of Christ and to reach beyond the body to grow the Kingdom:

*There are different kinds of gifts, but the same Spirit. There are different kinds of service, but the same Lord. There are different kinds of working, but the same God works all of them in all men. (1 Corinthians 12:4–6)*

Your Father has planted these gifts in you and in all other believers. He gives these gifts graciously, without measure. And he wants the gifts he has planted in you to grow. Be bold, then, to call on him to broaden and sharpen his gifts. You are a man of confidence. Christ dwells in you by faith. Ask him to enrich your thinking, speaking, and doing, confident that you lack nothing as you serve him until he returns in glory.

## *Deeper and Higher*
Rest assured in, and be motivated to serve by, the Spirit's gift to you and all Christians:

*All these are the work of one and the same Spirit, and he gives them to each one, just as he determines.*
1 Corinthians 12:11

## God @ Work

*During these next two days, reflect on the different ways
God is working in your life to draw you closer to him
in faith and bless you to be a blessing to others.*

**My Attitudes**
**My Character**
**My Finances**
**My Skills**
**My Spiritual Gifts**

*He will be like a tree planted by the water
that sends outs its roots by the stream.*
*Jeremiah 17:8*

*The man who trusts in the LORD . . .*
*[is] like a tree planted by the water. . . .*
*It does not fear when heat comes;*
*its leaves are always green.*
*Jeremiah 17:7–8*

God has planted you for every season.

Though you may feel burned,
       scorched by the pressures
       of this fallen, sinful world,
       don't be afraid; you are not alone.

Your Lord has chosen you
       and called you to be a man of faith,
       trusting in his guidance and protection.

He will equip you,
       growing you deeper and higher,
       that you may stand against the heat
       and flourish in his grace.

## Conformed to the Son

*As obedient children, do not conform to the evil desires you had when you lived in ignorance. But just as he who called you is holy, so be holy in all you do; for it is written: "Be holy, because I am holy." (1 Peter 1:14–16)*

Trees can wither when temperatures soar. Young trees, not yet fully formed, are especially vulnerable when the heat is on. Without plentiful water and relief from blistering sunlight, even mature trees can languish.

God calls you to be a "tree planted by water." Yet he knows you live and move and have your being in this fallen, sinful world. At times, the pressures to conform to the pattern of this world can overwhelm even mature Christians. The temptations of a world system broken and hostile to its creator can blister our souls and wilt our resolve.

Internet pornography. The temptation to cut corners at the office or in the shop. The belief that only those who compromise their principles get ahead. The frustrations inherent in accountability. The busy-ness that kills relationships. A critical attitude toward our children or others we mentor at home, church, or work. The list might soar into the hundreds . . .

When you feel the heat, the pressure to conform, what do you do? Do you turn to the cool, refreshing Living Water . . . Jesus Christ? If so, you need not fear when the heat comes. You have been grafted by grace onto his tree—his cross. You have been united with him in his life—the new life of his resurrection. You stand in the shade of his forgiveness, and you are daily rejuvenated—made whole, fresh, and green because of his mercy and love.

When the temperature rises in your life, your Father invites you into the seasonable weather of his promises in Christ. Stay close to him. Let the Lord conform you to his image for you—a mature, evergreen tree, seeking his holy will.

### Deeper and Higher
Hear your God's call:

*Do not conform any longer to the pattern of this world,*
*but be transformed by the renewing of your mind.*
*Then you will be able to test and approve what*
*God's will is—his good, pleasing and perfect will.*
Romans 12:2

## The Servant Way

*Do nothing out of selfish ambition or vain conceit, but in humility consider others better than yourselves. Each of you should look not only to your own interests, but also to the interests of others.*
*(Philippians 2:3–4)*

Ancient peoples had a ready label for harsh, oppressive, unjust rulers: ***tyrants!***

Tyranny was the rule of the ruler. What the ruler says, goes. What the ruler wants, he gets. No limitations. No boundaries. No checks and balances on his quest for power, authority, and greatness . . . none, that is, until another tyrant, more crafty and ruthless, comes along. Then the tyranny starts all over again.

Sometimes the heat of battle creates tyrants. Men fall prey to tyranny—their own. They issue orders. They make demands. They take what they want, when they want it, without considering the consequences of their actions and the damage they leave in their wake. They become dictators.

"Not so with you," Jesus encouraged his disciples. James and John, perhaps the other men too, had jockeyed for position—powerful, authoritative, and great positions—in Jesus' kingdom. But they missed the heart and character of his rule. Dwell on the Lord's words:

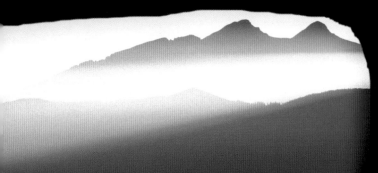

*Whoever wants to become great among you must be your servant, and whoever wants to be first must be slave of all. For even the Son of Man did not come to be served, but to serve, and to give his life as a ransom for many. (Mark 10:43–45)*

You may have power. You may have authority. You may be well positioned for status and reward in the future. But remember your Lord's call: "servant . . . slave . . . not come to be served, but to serve."

When the heat is on—to succeed at work, to finish projects at home, to make a difference in Little League baseball—you'll need the servant's attitude more than ever. The temptation will be tyranny. But ask your Father for the heart and character of his Son. Listen to your Savior. Learn from Christ's servant way. Invite him to rain down his grace to grow you as one who serves.

### Deeper and Higher
An attitude check for the man of God:

*Your attitude should be the same as that of Christ Jesus: Who, being in very nature God . . . made himself nothing, taking the very nature of a servant.*
*Philippians 2:5–7*

## Spiritual Desires

*Those who live according to the sinful nature have their minds set on what that nature desires; but those who live in accordance with the Spirit have their minds set on what the Spirit desires. (Romans 8:5)*

C. S. Lewis once wrote, "Every time you make a choice you are turning the central part of you, the part that chooses, into something a little different from what it was before."

The pressures of this world knock daily at your sinful nature. Anyone home? The reality is *yes*. Inside you, as the apostle Paul describes, is a residue, leftovers of sorts, of the man you once were. The apostle Paul reminds us, "There is no difference, for all have sinned and fall short of the glory of God" (Romans 3:22–23). That was your identity. That describes the man you were before the lavish, transforming grace of your Father in the gift of his Son.

Before: *There is no one righteous, not even one; there is no one who understands, no one who seeks God. All have turned away, they have together become worthless. (Romans 3:10–12)*

After: *Don't you know that all of us who were baptized into Christ Jesus were baptized into his death? We were therefore buried with him through baptism into death in order that, just as Christ was raised from the dead through the glory of the Father, we too may live a new life. (Romans 6:3–4)*

Within you, just as within every other Christian who has ever lived, the new, Spirit-given nature battles with the old, sin-stained nature. And the Spirit is serious! He desires to draw you to Christ. He wills to plant you firmly in the Word so that by his Spirit alive in every

part of you—roots, trunk, branches, even leaves—you bear abundant fruit. He wants every choice you make to turn you away from the old, sinful nature and toward a higher, deeper relationship with your Lord.

Ask your Father today to renew your desires so that they reflect the Holy Spirit's desires. He will help you choose new life.

### Deeper and Higher
Ready to follow? Fall in step with the Spirit:

*The fruit of the Spirit is love, joy, peace, patience, kindness, goodness, faithfulness, gentleness and self-control. Against such things there is no law. Those who belong to Christ Jesus have crucified the sinful nature with its passions and desires.*
Galatians 5:22–24

## A New Leaf

*Clothe yourselves with compassion, kindness, humility, gentleness and patience. Bear with each other and forgive whatever grievances you may have against one another. Forgive as the Lord forgave you. (Colossians 3:12–13)*

You get burned in a relationship. Someone scorches you at work. What do you feel? White-hot anger!

Heat seems to go naturally with anger. When the heat's on, how do you respond? Do you rage inside? Do you inwardly simmer and boil with resentment and hatred, waiting for the right moment to let off steam? Or do you blow your top and pour down rivers of molten lava—words and actions—that threaten to consume everyone in the path?

The tree that God has planted "does not fear when heat comes." It has leaves—green leaves—to shield and nourish it. And the Spirit desires to shade you from the heat of anger as he nurtures your life in Christ. Listen to the apostle James:

*My dear brothers, take note of this: Everyone should be quick to listen, slow to speak and slow to become angry, for man's anger does not bring about the righteous life that God desires. (James 1:19–20)*

What does a tree do to shade itself and to find nourishment during the heat of summer days? It "clothes" itself with leaves. Branches bloom and leaves blossom, not simply to make the tree stately and beautiful, but for shade, for sustenance, and to provide a mechanism by which it can constantly exchange bad for good, carbon dioxide for oxygen.

Of course, God "clothes" the trees with leaves. He creates and preserves all things. And your Maker has also promised to clothe you by his grace with his righteous life. He shows compassion, kindness, humility, gentleness, patience, and forgiveness to you in Christ's cross. This mercy then makes it possible for you to work through your anger, release your anger, and express your anger—when that's appropriate—in a healthy, constructive way. He will put on you the new nature of your life in Christ.

Angry today? Ask your Father to help you trust him to guide and protect you through the heat.

### *Deeper and Higher*
Contemplate the stately beauty of God's love flowing through you as you think about Paul's concluding words in Colossians:

*Over all these virtues put on love,*
*which binds them all together in perfect unity.*
Colossians 3:14

## Welcome Back

*For he himself is our peace, who has made the two one and has destroyed the barrier, the dividing wall of hostility . . . to create in himself one new man out of the two, thus making peace, and in this one body to reconcile both of them to God through the cross. (Ephesians 2:14–16)*

The hot, harmful breath of conflict blows all too frequently through relationships. Perhaps through yours, too. Perhaps even today, you have experienced a painful disagreement. Or maybe it was worse than that; maybe it was a fierce, agonizing fight with someone you work with, someone you live with, or someone you

usually sit close to in church. You've parted ways. You've stopped talking. You have no plans and you foresee no reason, no reason ever, to make contact or to seek reconciliation.

*He came to his senses.* That's what Jesus says about the younger son in the story he told about the prodigal. The boy knew he was wrong. He knew he had hurt his dad. But he trusted that his father would forgive and welcome him home.

This son wanted what we all want—reconciliation with the Father who gives us life and breath. So first he spoke to his own heart: "I will set out and go back to my father and say to him: Father, I have sinned against heaven and against you" (Luke 15:18).

Reconciliation begins with a step: *I will set out.* When the heat of conflict lingers in your life, take the first step: "Heavenly Father, I have sinned against you." Ask your Father's forgiveness. He has reconciled you in his Son and will welcome you home again and again to his mercy in your Lord Jesus.

Then step toward others. Ask your Father to give you strength. Call on him for wisdom to know where, how, to go forward. Pray that he opens a door . . . for the relationship to be restored and renewed.

Trust his Word: You are like a tree planted by water. You need not fear the heat of this day, for in Christ your leaves are green.

### *Deeper and Higher*
Listen tenderly, obediently to the Father's appeal:

*We are therefore Christ's ambassadors, as though God were making his appeal through us. We implore you on Christ's behalf: Be reconciled to God.*
*2 Corinthians 5:20*

## Pressure to . . .

*During these next two days, reflect on the different ways*
*God is working in you so that you may stand firm in*
*Christ throughout all seasons of your life.*

**Conform to This World**
**Dominate Others**
**Satisfy Personal Desires**
**Lose Control**
**Prolong Conflict**

*The man who trusts in the LORD . . . [is] like a tree*
*planted by the water. . . . It does not fear when heat*
*comes; its leaves are always green.*
*Jeremiah 17:7–8*

*The man who trusts in the LORD . . . [is] like a tree planted by the water. . . . It does not fear when heat comes; its leaves are always green. It has no worries in a year of drought and never fails to bear fruit.*
*Jeremiah 17:7–8*

God has planted you
        for the dry spells every man faces.

Though you feel parched and drained at times,
        don't be anxious:
        you are not alone.

Your Lord has watered you with his Word
        and supplies his wisdom
        and strength for you to be a man of faith.

He will rain down his grace on you,
        growing you deeper and higher,
        that you may be richly satisfied
        as you put your trust in him.

# Living Water

*Jesus answered, "Everyone who drinks this water will be thirsty again, but whoever drinks the water I give him will never thirst. Indeed, the water I give him will become in him a spring of water welling up to eternal life." (John 4:13–14)*

In a year of drought, Jeremiah assures us, the man of faith has no worries. This prophet knew firsthand the bleak reality of dry, desolate days. At one point in his mission to God's people, Jeremiah received a word from the Lord "concerning the drought" that ravaged his nation (Jeremiah 14:1). The nation's pain was real; tears and pleas for mercy flowed from the people of Judah as they suffered from lack of water, lack of food, and lack of hope.

In times of drought still today, we have every *human* reason to be anxious, because water is life and life is fragile. We have reason to be anxious, that is, unless we drink continually from the water that Jesus gives. That water is *living* water.

Are you thirsty, dried out, anxious? Jesus offers you a drink—a long, satisfying drink from a spring that wells up to eternal life. In him you have no lasting drought, no permanent lack, because he can and freely does pour out living water to refresh you, even in your driest, most desolate days.

The tree God has planted you to be "has no worries in a year of drought," Jeremiah assures you. Not that you'll escape drought conditions in your life. Not that you'll always steer clear of those arid, seemingly barren patches every man faces.

Notice exactly what the prophet says: you'll have *no worries*— no ultimate, permanent worries. You'll stand firm and tall in the confidence that your Father has called you by name and chosen you to be a man who lives by faith. You can trust his promise to work in you and through you to bear the fruit of the Spirit in all the seasons of your life.

When dry, desolate days overtake you, drink deeply. Drink often. Drink the water that Jesus pours out for you.

### Deeper and Higher
Ask the Spirit to refresh you as Christ has promised:

*If anyone is thirsty, let him come to me and drink.*
*Whoever believes in me, as the Scripture has said,*
*streams of living water will flow from within him.*
John 7:37–38

## Thirsty for God

*O God, you are my God, earnestly I seek you; my soul thirsts for you, my body longs for you, in a dry and weary land where there is no water. (Psalm 63:1)*

Trees suffer in drought. Even mature, resilient trees are affected by prolonged dry weather. Leaves and bark show early signs of deprivation. Prolonged drought can take a severe toll on the hardiest of oaks and pines and maples. Trunk rings prove it.

In Psalm 63, David compares the hurt he's feeling to a time of prolonged drought. Alone, in the desert, he had no one to turn to, no one to hold onto. He felt loss. He felt lost. He describes his longing for water where none may be found. Thirsty to the roots of his being, David was desperate for God to plant him beside the water, to irrigate him with a Father's life-giving presence.

Deep hurt makes us thirst in this same way. We ache for something that will dampen the pain. We long for even a moment's relief. We yearn for someone who knows how to diminish our grief, just a little.

You may have been touched by hurt and loss. You can still see events playing out: In your own home. Or on the job. Or in your doctor's office. Like David, you're thirsty inside. Like David, you long for water, for something to turn to and hold onto in the dry and dreary land you've entered.

From his desert place, David said to his Father, "My soul clings to you; your right hand upholds me" (Psalm 63:8). From your own desert place right now, you can trust this same truth. Now's the time to grab hold of your Father's life-giving presence. Now's the time to tighten your grip on his promises. Repeat King David's words to your King Jesus:

*Lord, you are my God; I seek you in my hurt. My soul thirsts for your compassion; my body longs for your healing touch. I cling to you, Lord. Hold me tightly in your gracious hands.*

### Deeper and Higher
Now confess this truth with David:

*Because your love is better than life,*
*my lips will glorify you.*
*I will praise you as long as I live,*
*and in your name I will lift up my hands.*
*Psalm 63:3–4*

## Balanced and Whole

*Like a cedar of Lebanon he will send down his roots; his young shoots will grow. His splendor will be like an olive tree, his fragrance like a cedar of Lebanon. (Hosea 14:5–6)*

*Tough and fragrant.* It's an unusual combination. Yet in biblical times cedar wood was prized for both its durability and its sweet smell. Merchants and craftsmen tapped cedars for resins and oils and then produced anointments and perfumes. Solomon bartered with the king of Tyre for cedars from Lebanon. He devoted the wood, with its rich finish and long-lasting aroma, to building the Lord's temple (1 Kings 5).

Through his prophet Hosea, the Lord calls Israel a "cedar." He sees his people as both tough and fragrant. He's planted them. He's caused their roots to spread out deep and wide. He sees in his people the splendor of an olive tree, highly valued in the ancient world as a symbol of peace and happiness. He's fashioned his beloved son Israel like a "cedar," because this provides a perfect combination of qualities to accomplish his will and purposes.

What combination—usual, interesting, or suitable—is the Lord planting in you? Your Father may desire to give your life balance. He may want to work in you a symmetry, a harmony and consistency you may need in the future as you serve him. Perhaps he's building in you deep conviction, tempered by compassion. Or perhaps passion, moderated by patience.

No matter what the mix you need, your Father knows how to balance you, how to water and cultivate just exactly the gifts you need.

Some traits, some qualities may lie dormant right now. You may need a soaking rain and healthy nutrients from God's Word to enable you to finish a project with excellence or make a positive impression on a client or manager. Whatever you lack for the work and witness to which your Father has called you, he will provide. He is growing you into a mighty cedar—valuable, balanced, and whole. He will grant you wisdom and give you all you need to "bear fruit" in abundance, for his glory and your good.

### *Deeper and Higher*
As you call on your God, take comfort in his reply:

*I will answer him and care for him.*
*I am like a green pine tree;*
*your fruitfulness comes from me.*
Hosea 14:8

## Free and Flexible

*Though I am free and belong to no man, I make myself a slave to everyone, to win as many as possible. . . . I have become all things to all men so that by all possible means I might save some. I do all this for the sake of the gospel, that I may share in its blessings. (1 Corinthians 9:19, 22–23)*

The trunk of a tree rarely moves. But branches do. Branches move daily as they are touched by gentle breezes and swayed by gusty winds. Branches dip and bend when feathery robins huddle in winter and plump squirrels frolic in summer. Branches are the "give-and-take" part of trees. Bouncing and swaying, branches and their leaves are poetry in motion—trees on the move.

Paul considered himself a man on the move, a branch connected to the Tree of Life. Literally, he traveled thousands of miles to share the Good News of Christ. Figuratively, he moved daily— sometimes subtly, sometimes dramatically—among all kinds of people. Jews and Gentiles. Slaves and rich merchants. Government officials and greedy swindlers. He could dip and bend to accommodate new settings and specific needs.

But the "trunk" of his faith never moved. He never compromised on God's Word. He was free and flexible in his ministry, but immovable on the saving truth of the Gospel. By his candid admission, he gives and takes, all for "the sake of the gospel," that by grace he might share the Lord's infinite blessings with many others.

The tree that God has made you to be stands free and flexible. You're released from sin, the fear of death, and the power of the devil. Jesus has unshackled you and planted you in his love. And he allows you to live in the "give-and-take" of his Gospel, to become, under his leadership, "all things to all men." You're free to move forward, even in a drought, as you bear fruit in all your relationships.

Put your anxiety behind you today. See the doors your Father opens. Walk through, trusting his guidance.

### *Deeper and Higher*
Meditate on God's exhortation:

*Be very careful, then, how you live—*
*not as unwise but as wise,*
*making the most of every opportunity,*
*because the days are evil.*
*Understand what the Lord's will is.*
Ephesians 5:15–17

## Fruitful Branches

*[Jesus said,] "I am the true vine, and my
Father is the gardener. He cuts off every branch in me
that bears no fruit, while every branch that does bear fruit
he prunes so that it will be even more fruitful." (John 15:1–2)*

It's no surprise that the prophets, apostles, and our Lord himself
all speak often about fruit, about fruitful trees and branches.
Almond, apricot, date, fig, olive, and pomegranate trees and
shrubs provided groceries for every family during Bible times.
Branches laden with fruit played a vital economic role in each
village marketplace and in many industries—farming,
manufacturing, international trade.

Ask a fruit grower, and he'll affirm the Bible's deep insight.
The process of growth in orchard and garden mirrors that
process in many other dimensions, the spiritual realm in
particular. In the Upper Room that Thursday evening before
his death, Jesus used a familiar picture of fruit-bearing to
convey profound truths about true discipleship:

*Remain in me, and I will remain in you. No branch can bear
fruit by itself; it must remain in the vine. Neither can you bear
fruit unless you remain in me. (John 15:4)*

Jesus is the "true vine," the trunk of the tree the Father has
planted. He is the genuine, permanent, eternal Son of God.
You are his branch. He has saved you, grafted you into his saving
death and resurrection.

His selfless act of sacrifice, his death on the tree of the cross in payment for each one of your sins, has sown new life in you. Now your Father, the true gardener, is filling that life with buds and then with abundant, generous, and luscious fruit, pruning you as he sees fit, to make you even more fruitful.

In every season, even during the dry spells, you trust your Father to make your fruit grow. And you have the privilege of asking, "Make me more fruitful!"

### Deeper and Higher
Hear the Living Vine again:

*I am the vine; you are the branches.*
*If a man remains in me and I in him,*
*he will bear much fruit;*
*apart from me you can do nothing.*
John 15:5

# The Dry Spells

*During the next two days, reflect on the different ways God is working in you so that you may stand firm in Christ through all the seasons of your life.*

**My Lord's Living Water**
**Hurt and Loss**
**Balance**
**Flexibility**
**Fruitful Branches**

*The man who trusts in the LORD . . . [is] like a tree planted by the water. It does not fear when heat comes; its leaves are always green. It has no worries in a year of drought and never fails to bear fruit.*
*Jeremiah 17:7–8*

*Blessed is the man who trusts in the LORD, whose confidence is in him. He will be like a tree planted by the water that sends out its roots by the stream. It does not fear when heat comes; its leaves are always green. It has no worries in a year of drought and never fails to bear fruit.*
**Jeremiah 17:7–8**

God truly has planted you.

And he will tend you and harvest your fruit
    all the days of your life.

He will bless you and keep you.

He will make his face shine on you to make you grow
    deeper and higher
    as you follow your Lord and Savior.

Trust him. He is your faithful God.

## A Blessed Man

*Blessed is the man who does not walk in the counsel of the wicked. . . .*
*He is like a tree planted by streams of water, which yields its fruit in*
*season and whose leaf does not wither. (Psalm 1:1, 3)*

Sound familiar? Jeremiah was not the only biblical writer to
portray the man of faith as a tree planted by water.

The book of Psalms begins on a note that echoes through all
the other 149 songs, poems, and prayers that follow. Psalm 1 sets
the tone, points the way, making a bold foundational statement.
If we were to paraphrase, we might say, "Blessed is the man in a
living faith relationship with the Lord."

Jeremiah agrees! His words have now become familiar: *Blessed*
*is the man who trusts in the LORD, whose confidence is in him.*

Consider yourself blessed today. Planted by God. Green in the
summer's heat. Fruitful even in the dry season. Jeremiah's
faithful words describe you, a man loved by God, called by
God, equipped by God, and sent forth to serve your God.

But know that *blessed* means much more than "staying cool
under fire." To be blessed means more than merely enjoying
the multiplication of possessions, status, position, or authority.
Jeremiah follows all of Scripture in using the word *blessed* to
mean primarily enjoying a relationship of favor with the
Lord himself:

> Blessed is he
>> whose transgressions are forgiven,
>> whose sins are covered.
>
> Blessed is the man
>> whose sin the LORD does not count against him
>> and in whose spirit is no deceit.
>>> *(Psalm 32:1–2)*

God looks on you as his very own son—what a blessing!
He regards you as forgiven and blameless—what a blessing!
Speaking from his heart, he declares you holy and perfect in
the cross of Jesus Christ—what a blessing!

You belong to God himself as his very own chosen possession.
He's seated you with Christ in his glory and given you authority
to serve in his name.

You are a blessed man . . . a man of faith!

### Deeper and Higher
Another psalm of trust to remember:

*I am like an olive tree
flourishing in the house
of God; I trust in
God's unfailing love
for ever and ever.*
*Psalm 52:8*

## My Health and Salvation

*Then the angel showed me the river of the water of life. . . .*
*On each side of the river stood the tree of life, bearing twelve crops*
*of fruit, yielding its fruit every month. And the leaves of the tree*
*are for the healing of the nations. (Revelation 22:1–2)*

Trees suggest many wonderful associations in the Bible. One is
health and healing. As John's vision in the book of Revelation
draws to a close, he sees the tree of life—Christ's own planting in
his eternal kingdom—bestow healing on all who trust him for
salvation. No more pain, no more suffering, no more death in
the heavenly city. The Lamb of God makes all things new.

God regards your own health and healing with fatherly concern.
He encourages you to manage your body, mind, and spirit as a
steward of his gifts. And when your health falters and you need
healing, he invites you to ask for his goodness and mercy,
according to his will in Christ. In sickness or in health,
he calls you to trust in him.

Your Lord holds your well-being in his hands. Man of faith,
listen! Take to heart your Savior's promise in Ezekiel 17:22–24:

*This is what the Sovereign LORD says:*

*I myself will take a shoot from the very top of a cedar and plant it;*
*I will break off a tender sprig from its topmost shoots*
*and plant it on a high and lofty mountain. . . . (He means you.)*

*On the mountain heights of Israel I will plant it; it will produce branches and bear fruit and become a splendid cedar.* . . . (The Lord will make you effective where he plants you.)

*Birds of every kind will nest in it; they will find shelter in the shade of its branches.* . . . (He'll make you a blessing to others, and you'll share cheerfully from your abundance.)

*All the trees of the field will know that I the Lord bring down the tall tree and make the low tree grow tall. I dry up the green tree and make the dry tree flourish.* (Everyone will know that your Father orders all your days.)

### Deeper and Higher
Attention, please:

*I the Lord have spoken, and I will do it.*
Ezekiel 17:24

## My Joy and Praise

*Let the heavens rejoice, let the
earth be glad; let the sea resound,
and all that is in it; let the fields
be jubilant, and everything in
them. Then all the trees of the
forest will sing for joy.
(Psalm 96:11–12)*

God convenes a grand
celebration for his creation.
The heavens are present; earth's
accounted for. The sea joins in.
The fields wouldn't miss it for
the world.

Who leads the singing?
*The trees!*

Can you imagine the resonant
bass tones that the mighty oaks
contribute to the chorus? Can
you hear the balsams joining
in as tenors? From all around
the earth the voices blend
together . . . cherry trees and
chestnuts, hawthorns and
hickories, pear trees and
poplars . . . all in joyful
praise to their Lord!

the duty to raise your voice, united with the chorus that sings praise to the one and only Creator. And the melody you add is the song of the church, the song of thousands upon thousands, ten thousand times ten thousand, who worship the Father, the Son, and the Holy Spirit:

*Worthy is the Lamb, who was slain, to receive power and wealth and wisdom and strength and honor and glory and praise! . . . To him who sits on the throne and to the Lamb, be praise and honor and glory and power, for ever and ever! (Revelation 5:12–13)*

Your Father summons you to praise. By his design, you are invited to the grand celebration each week. Sunday, Wednesday, Saturday—whenever you gather with God's people to lift your voice in thanksgiving, to hear his Word, and to sink your roots more deeply into the fertile soil of his Good News.

As a man of faith, take seriously the Lord's call to worship. Set an example for your family . . . for the children in your life . . . for your friends who may at times waver in their commitment to their local church family. Join in the song: "Worthy is Christ the Lamb!"

### *Deeper and Higher*
As a tree of God's planting, picture this as you
prepare to celebrate:

*You will go out in joy and be led forth in peace;
the mountains and hills will burst into song before you,
and all the trees of the field will clap their hands.*
Isaiah 55:12

# My Days and Years

*Remember the former things, those of long ago; I am God, and there is no other; I am God, and there is none like me. I make known the end from the beginning, from ancient times, what is still to come. (Isaiah 46:9–10)*

Over 1,500 years. That's the age of some sequoias!

Sequoia trees are perhaps the most fascinating trees in North America. Located in the coastal regions of California and Oregon, sequoias tower over all other species of trees. They can grow to a height of over 300 feet. Their trunks range from 10 to 20 feet in diameter. Nothing else really compares. These "giants" of the earth stand proud and tall as testaments to the God who reigns from everlasting to everlasting.

Yet sequoias only dimly reflect the reality of the grandeur that blazes from Isaiah's words: *I am God, and there is no other; I am God, and there is none like me.*

The Lord God commands time. He controls days and years. He makes beginnings. He chooses endings. From birth to death, all creation, including the lofty sequoia, lies in his hands, dependent on his care. He orders and sustains all life, from the dense forests of northern California to the wild sapling of a fig tree near Jerusalem. There is none like God.

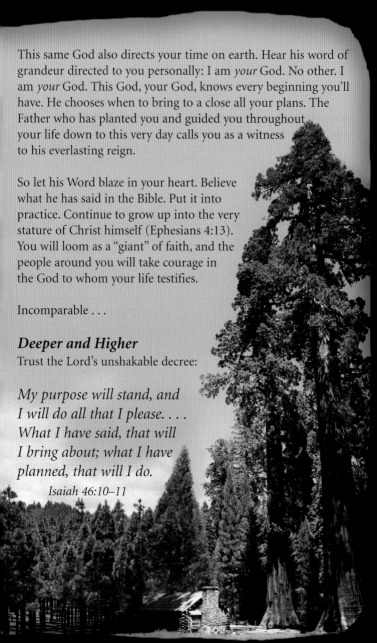

This same God also directs your time on earth. Hear his word of grandeur directed to you personally: I am *your* God. No other. I am *your* God. This God, your God, knows every beginning you'll have. He chooses when to bring to a close all your plans. The Father who has planted you and guided you throughout your life down to this very day calls you as a witness to his everlasting reign.

So let his Word blaze in your heart. Believe what he has said in the Bible. Put it into practice. Continue to grow up into the very stature of Christ himself (Ephesians 4:13). You will loom as a "giant" of faith, and the people around you will take courage in the God to whom your life testifies.

Incomparable . . .

### Deeper and Higher
Trust the Lord's unshakable decree:

*My purpose will stand, and*
*I will do all that I please. . . .*
*What I have said, that will*
*I bring about; what I have*
*planned, that will I do.*

  *Isaiah 46:10–11*

## My Focus

*I want to know Christ and the power of his resurrection and the fellowship of sharing in his sufferings, becoming like him in his death, and so, somehow, to attain to the resurrection from the dead. (Philippians 3:10–11)*

Having read the devotions in this booklet, you know the prophet Jeremiah a bit better than when you began. You know what he believed about God. You know what he cherished about faith and living in this world. But above all, you know he wants *all men* to know the living Lord.

To the day he died, Jeremiah remained focused on that. Perhaps as he closed his eyes for the last time on this earth, his final thoughts returned to the phrase he had proclaimed throughout his ministry: *Blessed is the man who trusts in the LORD, whose confidence is in him.*

Jeremiah was focused. He knew where his real life began and where it would end. God wants you, too, to have a clear focus for your life:

> To know Christ . . .
> the power of his *resurrection*
> the fellowship of sharing in his *sufferings*
> becoming like him in his *death*
> attaining to the *resurrection* from the dead.

The beginning of your real life is Christ's suffering, his death. By faith you are a partner, a "fellow" in his sacrifice for the sins of the world.

The ending of your real life is Christ's resurrection, his victory over death. His resurrection is power, God's power for you! By faith in his matchless triumph, you are assured of your own resurrection when Jesus comes back in glory.

He is the Lord you trust. In Jesus, and in Jesus alone, you've placed your confidence. Like Jeremiah, you have a focus, every day, through every planting and replanting, through times of heat and drought, through opportunities and setbacks. You are a man of faith. Now grow deeper and higher . . .

- Send your roots out, far and wide.
- Stand tall against the heat, in the drought.
- Drink deeply from the Living Water.
- And let the Spirit's fruit mature in you.

### *Deeper and Higher*
Focus on this tree . . . always:

*He himself bore our sins in his body on the tree,*
*so that we might die to sins and live for righteousness;*
*by his wounds you have been healed.*

*1 Peter 2:24*

## The Man Who Trusts the Lord

*During these next two days, reflect on the different ways God will work in your life to keep you a man of faith.*

**A Blessed Man**
**My Health and Salvation**
**My Joy and Praise**
**My Days and Years**
**My Focus**

*But blessed is the man who trusts in the LORD, whose confidence is in him. He will be like a tree planted by the water that sends out its roots by the stream. It does not fear when heat comes; its leaves are always green. It has no worries in a year of drought and never fails to bear fruit.*
*Jeremiah 17:7–8*

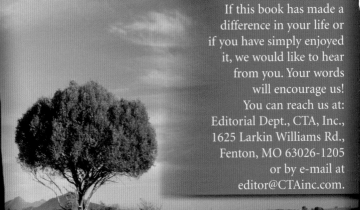

If this book has made a difference in your life or if you have simply enjoyed it, we would like to hear from you. Your words will encourage us! You can reach us at: Editorial Dept., CTA, Inc., 1625 Larkin Williams Rd., Fenton, MO 63026-1205 or by e-mail at editor@CTAinc.com.